Faith on the Edge Series

Heaven and Hell

The Edge of Eternity

Norbert Becker

CONCORDIA PUBLISHING HOUSE • SAINT LOUIS

3558 S. Jefferson Ave., St. Louis, MO 63118-3968
1-800-325-3040 • www.cph.org

Written by Norbert Becker; contributions by Edward Engelbrecht

Edited by Robert C. Baker

This publication may be available in braille, in large print, or on cassette tape for the visually impaired. Please allow 8 to 12 weeks for delivery. Write to the Library for the Blind, 7550 Watson Rd., St. Louis, MO 63119-4409; call toll-free 1-888-215-2455; or visit the Web site: www.blindmission.org.

Manufactured in the United States of America

2 3 4 5 6 7 8 9 10 13 12 11 10 09 08 07 06 05

CONTENTS

About This Series

In the past science served as a stepchild to alchemy, a handmaiden of theology, and a tool of industry. At the beginning of the twentieth century, science took on a new role. Science became the answer to all humankind's problems. The priests and priestesses of science vested in white lab coats, prophesied through their theories, and consecrated each new discovery or invention. Humans marveled.

In response to these wonders, a new type of literature arose—science fiction, which sometimes warned us about the maddening pace of technology. The robot would replace the human worker. Nuclear fallout would devastate life on earth. Science would solve human problems, but perhaps by doing away with people's humanity.

Today, people remain thankful for science. But they also recognize that science does not hold all the answers. In fact, they see that science can raise more questions than it answers, driving people on further quests for understanding, truth, and contentment.

The Faith on the Edge Bible study series tracks the progress of science and people's fascinations and fears about science. Each session introduces a contemporary topic, summarizes what science has to say about it, and then provides biblical answers and guidance so that you can face the future with the wisdom and confidence that only God can provide through His Word.

Student Introduction

Attaboy, Clarence!

—the character "George Bailey" in the film It's a Wonderful Life

Popular misconceptions about the afterlife run the gamut from abject denial (atheism, nihilism, annihilationism) to the fanciful: clockmakers like Clarence become angels after death, earning their heavenly wings through earthly deeds (hyper-spiritualism).

Some people ask quite glibly, "How can a loving God send good people to hell?" as if the reality of evil logically justified the denial of God's existence. Perhaps those asking such a question err not by going too far, but by not going far enough. We must also ponder: "How can a just God allow sinners into heaven?"

That question can be answered only in Jesus Christ, true God and true man. By His bloody cross and empty tomb we are fully forgiven. Baptized into Him, our bodies will be raised to perfection and life on the Last Day. Through the deposit of His Spirit we now yearn for the new heaven and the new earth.

Jesus Christ is God in flesh and blood. The two natures of the one Christ remind us of the dangers of pitting one aspect of our faith against another. By maintaining the tension between what only appears to be a contradiction, the Clarence of film can become the Clarence of faith. The erstwhile clockmaker enjoys heaven because of God's grace in Christ, and will be resurrected in his perfect, human body. No wings are necessary.

Little Zuzu's bell still rings. But this time its cheerful sound reminds us not of rewards outside the body, but of God's grace in Jesus Christ experienced in the body—here and now and in the life of the world to come.

The Editor

CHAPTER ONE

There Is a Heaven—Really!

A young Christian mother lay dying of cancer in a hospital. It was obvious that she was in great pain. Her unbelieving husband listened as the pastor ministered to her. The husband's only comment was, "Nobody ought to suffer like that!" Indirectly, he was saying, "Where is your God now?" The pastor could only respond: "This is why she loves her Savior. She knows that when mysteries and disappointments confront us in our earthly life, they cannot rob her of eternal life in heaven."

The wife's and the husband's views of suffering sharply contrasted because one believed in heaven and the other did not. This underscores the importance of our study on heaven. It points us to our need for the sure and clear promises God makes in His Word, which free us from all doubts and fears about the afterlife.

Some people have said that all we know about our future life in heaven is that everything is good. It is true that our knowledge about heaven is limited by (1) what God has chosen to reveal to us and (2) our limited understanding of spiritual things. Yet there's much that we can learn.

1. What are some things you know—and do not know—about heaven?

As you go through this study, you may be surprised at the large number of scriptural references about eternal life in heaven. Surely, God has reasons for revealing these things to us before we get there.

2. Read John 14:1–2 and Colossians 3:1–2. What are two ways that thinking of heaven can help you now?

Curious beings that we are, we may wish for more details about our future life in heaven. When some of our questions remain unanswered, we do well to focus on the chief purpose for which the Scriptures were given to us.

3. Read John 20:30–31. Why may a person be satisfied with what has and has not been revealed in the Bible?

Exploring Life after Death

Do we see a renewed interest in heaven in our times? Yes and no. Yes, because our society is beginning to realize that there must be life beyond what we see now. Some in the scientific community today accept the possibility of some kind of spirit world beyond the physical. However, we must also say *no* because society in general seems less and less interested in what the Bible says about the matter. Belief in some kind of afterlife is not necessarily the same as accepting the Christian teaching of heaven that is based on the authoritative Scriptures.

4. Read Romans 8:38–39, which is often heard at Christian funerals. What does it mean that God's love is stronger than death?

More and more we hear claims of near-death or after-death experiences indicating that human life is not limited to the body. Some claim to have hovered over their own body on an operating table.

5. Do these claims in any way relate to your belief in heaven? Discuss.

Charles Darwin's theory of evolution has convinced many people that humans are nothing more than a higher form of animal life. They have concluded that humans have no immortal soul and that there can be no resurrection of the body with eternal life in heaven. The Christian heaven is, therefore, often the object of ridicule by some intellectuals and skeptics.

6. Can you give examples of such ridicule in the media?

Jesus and the apostles emphasize that heaven is not merely something added to our Christian faith, but an essential part of it. If there is no afterlife, the unbelieving world is better off than we are.

7. Read Matthew 6:19–21 and 1 Corinthians 15:12–20. What do Jesus and Paul say about the importance of heaven in our faith?

Even though God has included so much about heaven in our Scriptures (The New Testament uses the term "eternal life" or "everlasting life" 66 times!), Christian beliefs in heaven have suffered some erosion in modern times. Surveys show that even some church members have doubts and are woefully ignorant of what the Bible teaches about heaven.

8. Automobiles often display Christian words and symbols as well as more mundane thoughts like "I'd rather be fishing." If we truly believe in heaven, why don't we display bumper stickers proclaiming, "I'd rather be in heaven"?

The apostle Paul gives us a good perspective for life here and now versus life in the hereafter.

9. Read the apostle Paul's thoughts in Philippians 1:22–26. Do you feel like he does? Why may you pray and hope for a longer life on earth?

Atheism dogmatically denies the existence of any supreme being apart from and outside of the physical universe. That denial precludes the assertion of divine revelation and any future life with God in heaven. Agnosticism does not explicitly deny the existence of deity, but rather asserts that any certain knowledge about the divine, or an afterlife, has not been reached. On the basis of ancient religious texts and traditions, those believing in reincarnation assert that, after death, a person's life force or soul transmigrates into other bodies—including plant or animal life.

10. How do these beliefs conflict with the Bible's teachings?

11. The Book of Revelation has much to say about heaven. Why should you receive these words and promises as God's truth? Read Revelation 1:1–3 and Revelation 22. What confidence and encouragement do they provide?

12. If doubts come to you regarding heaven, what can you learn from the apostle Paul in 2 Timothy 1:12? What plans have you made to put Paul's words into practice?

Heaven is real. God's Word is clear on this point. Life in Christ is eternal life. Don't be influenced by the unbelieving world that doesn't know Christ or His Word. Any doubts and fears you may have about the afterlife can be dispelled as you focus on God's sure promises.

Put your confidence in Jesus Christ. He promised that His truth will set you free. Remember that when your sins condemned you to hell, He put you on the road to heaven by His suffering, death, and resurrection. Prayerfully reflect on the "pictures of heaven" in this study and pray that your family, friends, and neighbors will be convinced, with you, of the glories awaiting all who trust in the Lord Jesus.

Words to Remember

I consider that the sufferings of this present time are not worth comparing with the glory that is to be revealed to us. Romans 8:18

CHAPTER TWO

Popular Misconceptions

The earth is full of misconceptions about heaven. Consider the following examples:

- Five-year-old Jenny came home from Sunday school with a puzzled look on her face: "Mommy, our teacher said that in heaven we'll all become angels. Will I have to wear those big wings?"

- Michelle was a high school honor student and was preparing excitedly for graduation evening. Her father had passed away tragically a few months before. Her mother assured her, "Your Daddy will be proud of you. I'm sure he'll be there to celebrate with you."
- Hoping to comfort a grieving friend, Terry said, "The Lord must have needed another angel in heaven. That's why He took your wife."

Examples like these are commonplace among Christians. Some misconceptions about the heavenly life are quite harmless, but others can be damaging to the faith. The Bible reveals all we need to know about heaven and urges us not to be deceived by human thoughts and imagination.

Down through the ages, Christian groups and individuals have offered many opinions about heaven. Many of them are interesting, some are strange, and others border on the bizarre. All of them go beyond what the Scriptures actually teach.

13. Glance quickly at the seven headings of this chapter. Which of these do you consider to be the most dangerous to the Christian faith? The least dangerous?

Heaven Is for Everybody

We have all heard it: "We're all heading for the same place." Like four golfers who tee off together, some go left, some go right, and others go down the middle of the fairway, but all end up on the green. "If 'God is love,'" (1 John 4:16) the thinking goes, "He must accept all of His creatures into heaven."

14. What does this wishful thinking forget about God? How does it disagree with God's revealed plan of salvation? Read 1 John 3:4–10 and John 3:16–18.

While there is one God, and we know that He loves all people, Scripture often speaks of pairs: believers and unbelievers, just and unjust, sheep and goats, angels and demons, God and Satan, heaven and hell. The division between heaven-bound and hell-bound people is not always clear to us in this life.

15. When will the division be clearly seen by all? Read Matthew 25:34–41.

16. On what basis will the Lord make this division?

Heaven Is for Good People

Many who realize that heaven is not for everyone fall into another trap—the belief that one earns heaven by being good. They mean those who are morally "good enough" but perhaps not perfect. Weighing the good against the bad, some will make the grade while others will not.

17. What is wrong about this seemingly reasonable thinking? Read Romans 3:22–24 and James 2:10.

The curse of this belief is that the person who believes it must live with constant uncertainty: What is "good enough" to get to heaven? Martin Luther, the great church reformer, languished under this cloud of doubt and fear until he discovered the liberating Gospel of Christ.

18. Read Ephesians 2:8–9 and Romans 3:22–24. How does anyone become good enough for heaven?

19. What happens to the Gospel of Christ when we try to work our way into heaven? Read Galatians 1:6–7.

Heaven Is on Earth

A heaven-related belief is held by some who wish to discredit the Christian belief in a real heaven. Denying that there is any afterlife, and realizing that good and evil should in some way be rewarded or punished, they theorize that we must create our own heaven or hell on earth.

20. Which Bible teaching about man's being is denied here? Read Genesis 1:27. How does the above opinion deny what God teaches about human life? What else does an "earthly" heaven or hell deny? Read Revelation 20:11–15.

Christians do experience a foretaste of heaven in their earthly life, but it is no substitute for the eternal life promised in the Bible.

Heaven Is Merely a Condition

Space travel and powerful telescopes have not yet located a heaven "out there." From this, some have concluded that heaven must be merely a "condition" or state of mind.

21. Did Jesus have anything to say about heaven being a real place? Read John 14:2–3.

Mysteries remain. Our resurrected and glorified bodies will be "spiritual" bodies like the body of the risen Christ. What kind of location does a spiritual body require? And where is this heaven located? The Scriptures speak of heaven as being "up." For example, Jesus ascended into heaven and will come down from heaven when He returns. Beyond that, heaven's location must remain a mystery.

From Heaven They Smile Down on Us

Not infrequently when a loved one has died and is missing an important event, we hear it said that the deceased "is here" or "is smiling down on us today." This view of the dead having intimate knowledge of every affair on earth may arise out of wishful thinking or sentimentality, but it cannot be supported by God's Word.

22. Do the Scriptures say anything about a dead person's knowledge of things on earth? Read Ecclesiastes 9:5 and Isaiah 63:16. On the other hand, Scripture does indicate that the martyrs in heaven do have some sense of what is happening on earth, and that the souls of the dead do express concern over the living. Read Revelation 6:9–10 and Luke 16:27. What are we to make of all these passages?

God could, of course, give saints in heaven a special vision of pleasant things on earth. Jesus once related an illustrative story to emphasize that we should not expect communication between heaven and earth. In Luke 16:19–30, a rich man in hell requested that a messenger be sent to his brothers on earth. The Lord did not fulfill his request.

23. Read Luke 16:29–31. How does heaven communicate with us earthlings?

In Heaven We Become Angels

You may have seen cartoons where people in heaven have sprouted wings and are lounging on puffy clouds. Or perhaps you have viewed the classic movie *It's a Wonderful Life*, in which the bungling angel, Clarence, struggles to earn his wings. Many believe that in heaven we become angels.

24. If we were to become angels, would this be a promotion or a demotion?

One cult claiming the name *Christian* goes even further. They teach that in heaven we can become gods. How absurd! Even becoming angels goes beyond what the Scriptures say. Angels are special creatures of God whose purpose is to serve His redeemed people.

25. What unique title and position is given to Christians in heaven? Read Romans 8:17.

26. In what angelic activities will you participate in heaven? See Revelation 5:11–14.

St. Peter Guards the Pearly Gates

The notion that St. Peter is the gatekeeper of heaven, admitting or rejecting applicants, is often expressed in jokes. But this teaching is misleading and damaging to some.

27. How may this notion of Peter at the pearly gates have arisen? Read Matthew 16:19.

In Revelation, the Bible describes twelve "pearly gates," not one gate. Twelve angels stand at these gates (21:12–13).

28. Read Matthew 25:34 and Revelation 20:11–12. Who decides which people enter heaven and which will not?

The manner of our entry into heaven does not seem important in the Bible. Neither is St. Peter responsible for our salvation. Our focus should always be on Him who is King of kings and Lord of lords.

29. Read John 10:7–10. How does this passage describe the role of "gatekeeper"?

As a student of God's Word, you should be able to sort out the truths and the untruths about heaven. Not all speculations about life in heaven undermine our saving faith, but even the "harmless" ones can detract from what the Scriptures actually teach. They should not be encouraged.

The most damaging misconceptions are those that do not recognize Jesus as the only way to the Father and the glories of heaven. Don't be deceived by those high-sounding philosophies that "all religions are good" and "we're all heading for the same place." Stay grounded in the biblical truth that, though Christ died for all, heaven is for those who know Him as the one who rescued them from sin, death, and hell by His death and resurrection.

Words to Remember

As the heavens are higher than the earth, so are My ways higher than your ways and My thoughts than your thoughts. Isaiah 55:9

CHAPTER THREE

Pictures of Heaven

In an elementary school religion class, the teacher announced: "Our study today is about heaven. I want each of you to draw a picture of something you expect to see or do when you are in heaven." Pictures submitted included angels, a crown, a playground, a flower garden, and many others. The teacher later singled out Kevin's drawing for comment: "Why did you draw the picture of a man?" Kevin's reply surprised everyone: "Because the best part of heaven will be that I get to see Jesus."

Kevin got it right. The best part of heaven is to see Jesus face–to–face and be in His presence forever. The Scriptures, however, do add a number of grand and glorious "pictures of heaven" that increase our joy of anticipation and our determination to remain faithful to our Lord.

Biblical pictures of heaven are necessarily given in terms of our earthly experience and cannot fully describe the future life. Depictions of heaven in religious paintings or films must be viewed with care, since they are based on the artists' imaginations.

30. What purpose might such paintings or films serve for you now? Read Romans 5:2 and 1 Corinthians 13:12.

Paradise

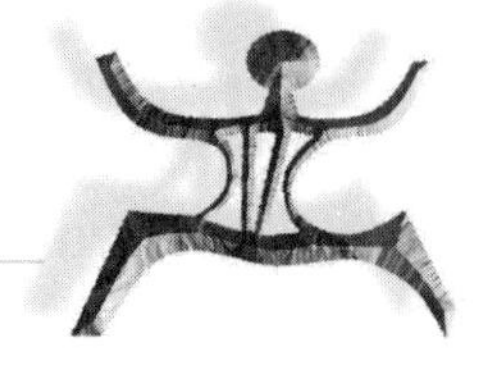

The term evokes images of all that we think of as the "good life" and easy living. The word occurs only three times in Scripture and was mentioned by Jesus Himself.

31. Read Luke 23:43. How much detail does Jesus give you about paradise here?

Paradise naturally causes us to think of the Garden of Eden where Adam and Eve lived close to God in a beautiful place. The advertising world has borrowed the word *paradise* to lure us to exotic places: resorts, golf courses, and South Sea islands. God's paradise will provide far greater pleasures—and without high prices, sand traps, or mosquitoes.

32. Read of Paul's experience in 2 Corinthians 12:2–4. Why couldn't Paul tell us more about paradise from this experience?

The word *paradise* originally meant a pleasure ground or park. The word *Eden* means "delight." You may picture heaven as a delightful park and still be surprised when you get there!

The Father's House

A most endearing picture of heaven is given by Jesus Himself in the upper room on the eve of His crucifixion.

33. Read John 14:1–3. What images are conjured up in your mind through this passage?

Jesus emphasizes the "hominess" of heaven—as a hymn points out: "Heav'n is my home" (*LW* 515, *TLH* 660).

In the original language, the word *rooms* (NIV) is not easily translated. (For example, the King James Version uses the word *mansions*) The typical construction of Israelite homes helps us understand the passage better. Israelite families usually dwelt in a collection of houses built around the first house erected by the head of the family. These homes were usually enclosed by a wall and shared a "compound" where the family members could work and play. This group of buildings was called "the house of . . ." followed by the father's name.

34. Read 1 Kings 12:21–26 about the rivalry between King Rehoboam and Jeroboam. How broadly might the ancient Israelites apply this picture of household/family?

The word for "rooms" conveys with certainty that there is enough space for all in the Father's glorious presence. Our focus in this picture should be on dwelling with our loving Father, rather than on any particular kind of structure.

The Holy City

This picture of heaven, extremely meaningful to the believers of Jesus' day, becomes meaningful for us as we realize that we are the "new Israel" of which the Bible speaks.

35. Read Revelation 21:2–4. Do you think this passage should be taken literally?

Jerusalem epitomized glory and honor and power to the early Christians. The temple there stood for God's presence, His dwelling with His people. This must also be our focus. Do we expect—as some do—that we shall be literally walking on streets of gold (not a very comfortable walk)? Or riding up to the new Jerusalem on the space shuttle?

A better thought: In the new Jerusalem, we shall be in the company of Abraham, Moses, Ruth, David, Isaiah, Mary, and other believers as God dwells among us.

"Rest"

Rest—another emotionally charged picture of heaven. Jesus promised this rest to all who come to Him in faith.

36. Read His beautiful promise in Matthew 11:25–30. What is the essence of this rest as promised here?

The rest and peace we humans crave begins on earth but is far from perfect until we reach the heavenly home. Ironically, the perfect life begins at death for believers.

37. Read Revelation 14:13, which is often heard at funerals. Why are those who die "in the Lord" called "blessed"?

A believer's rest is more than relief from earthly suffering.

38. Read Ecclesiastes 12:7. What kind of rest do you begin to experience at death?

Rest in heaven is a perfect peace, but we should not equate this rest with inactivity. Human beings were made to be active. Adam and Eve in the garden were not simply swinging in hammocks. They were to tend the garden.

39. What activity does the Bible tell us we will enjoy in heaven? Read Revelation 5:9–14.

Forever with the Lord

There are many unknowns about life in heaven, but we do know its most important feature.

40. Read 1 Thessalonians 4:17–18. What does the apostle Paul emphasize about heaven?

The Lord's presence with us on earth is real and powerful, but it cannot be compared with the joy of being with Him in heaven.

41. What does Paul contrast in Philippians 1:21–26?

42. What is his conclusion (v. 25)?

The Spirit's presence among us, and even within us, comforts and sustains us now, but we are still hounded by evil forces. Evil cannot exist in God's presence in heaven. God is light. God is love. "Forever with the Lord" is the essence of heaven!

The Crown of Life

In heaven, God's people wear crowns. These are variously described as a "crown of righteousness," a "crown of glory," and a "crown of life." Even if these crowns are literal, they still have symbolic meaning, just like earthly crowns.

43. Read 2 Timothy 4:8; 1 Peter 5:4; and Revelation 2:10. What does it means to wear these crowns?

On earth, our instinctive desire to be recognized and honored is often thwarted. Others rule over us and sometimes oppress us. In heaven we will be "on top of the world." All of God's people will be kings and queens. The King of kings will share His honor with us. Whether there are specific ways in which we shall share in His authority and lordship remains to be seen.

44. In biblical times, a crown was also given to athletes. Read 1 Corinthians 9:25. How is our crown superior to theirs?

I Shall Know Fully

45. One of the delights of heaven will be complete knowledge. What are some mysteries you look forward to having solved there?

46. Read 1 Corinthians 13:12 and 1 John 3:2. What improvements will be made in your mind? To what will your eyes be treated?

Like our bodies, our minds will somehow be glorified to resemble the mind of God. Most important will be our knowledge of God Himself, who now often seems far away and mysterious. It is very possible, of course, that questions we have now may seem outdated and irrelevant in His glorious presence.

A Spiritual Body

In the previous lesson we introduced the idea that God saves us in body and soul. At committal services in the cemetery, we often hear from 1 Corinthians 15 about the "spiritual body."

47. What thoughts does such language evoke for you?

48. Read 1 Corinthians 15:42–44 where Paul struggles to describe what is indescribable. Summarize his thoughts.

The bodies we now see are flesh and blood, but spirits are invisible. The Scriptures insist that flesh and blood cannot inherit the kingdom of God, yet our resurrected bodies will be real individual bodies. The term "spiritual body" seems contradictory to our way of thinking.

49. Read Philippians 3:20–21. How should you picture your heavenly body?

The pictures and descriptions of your future life in heaven are overwhelming. Ponder and reflect on them often. Let them sustain and comfort you when the going gets rough in your earthly life. Picture the glories of heaven, and you will want to remain faithful unto death and receive the crown of life!

Anticipating heaven's glories will draw you closer to your Savior, who reminds us that we must pass through much tribulation to enter into the kingdom of God (John 16:33; Romans 8:35–39). Through His own suffering and death on earth, Christ opened the kingdom of heaven to all believers. Look forward to spending an eternity with Him!

Words to Remember

No eye has seen, nor ear heard, nor the heart of man imagined, what God has prepared for those who love Him. 1 Corinthians 2:9

CHAPTER FOUR

That Other Place

Little Julie came home with a disturbed look on her face: “Mommy, I saw two guys arguing on the street and one guy told the other one to ‘Go to hell.’ Isn’t hell a terrible place to be—or was he just joking?”

Her concerned mother tried to explain: “He must have been very angry and didn’t know what else to say. Maybe he doesn’t really know what hell is.”

This little incident points up the general ignorance that prevails concerning the seriousness of hell. Even Christians often need reminders or refreshers on this point. The Bible is clear and explicit on the reality of hell. We cannot think of heaven without being aware of “that other place.”

Hell

Hell is one of those four-letter words we hear bandied about glibly and carelessly.

50. What might this careless use of the word *hell* seem to say about people's belief in or understanding of hell?

51. We seldom hear serious discussions about hell even among believers. Perhaps not even from the pulpit. Why?

The Reality of Hell

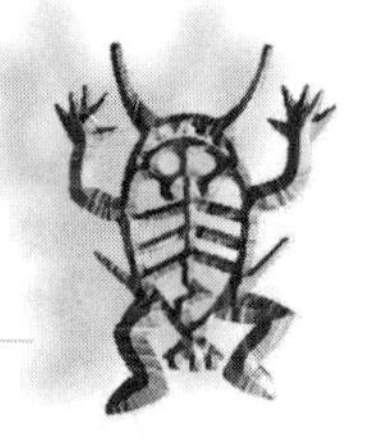

Expressions like "war is hell" may indicate that for some people, hell is nothing more than intense suffering on earth. Even some who believe in a real heaven cannot accept a real hell. God is love, the argument goes, and could not punish anyone eternally. But this argument overlooks another important attribute of God.

52. Read Deuteronomy 5:7–15. What does this tell us about God's personality, in addition to His great love?

53. Read John 3:18. How do we answer those who argue that "God would never send anyone to hell"?

Rather than argue "hell vs. no hell," we do well to examine what God in His wisdom and for our good has revealed to us in His Word. Unpleasant as the subject may be, the Scriptures are clear on the matter. The Bible uses the word *hell* about sixty times. Even Jesus, loving and forgiving as He is, did not hesitate to describe hell.

54. Read Matthew 25:41–46. What does Jesus teach about hell? Why do you suppose a loving Jesus would speak so bluntly about hell?

55. God has revealed the horror of hell for the sake of both unbelievers and believers. What purpose does this serve for unbelievers? Read Matthew 10:28.

56. Christians need to be reminded of the reality of hell for a twofold purpose. Read Ephesians 2:3–5 and Romans 10:13–14 and find the two purposes.

What, Where, and When

As with heaven, the Scriptures can only speak of hell in human terms and pictures. Spiritual things are still beyond our comprehension. We do know that the essence of hell is total separation from God's love and care. Though unbelievers do not receive God's Spirit, God does not totally abandon them during their earthly life. He still shows mercy to them in many ways. In hell, residents will learn what it is to be totally without God's love and care.

57. Read Acts 2:38–39. What does God urge unbelievers to do now?

58. The Scriptures refer to hell using four different terms, some of which are not easily understood. There are two common descriptions or pictures of hell. They depict terrible suffering. We read about the first in Matthew 25:41 above. Now read Matthew 8:12. How is intense suffering pictured in each of these passages?

The fire picture is most commonly used today. Five times, the Book of Revelation graphically refers to being thrown into a "lake of fire." How literally we should take these pictures? Since we are dealing with spiritual mysteries, caution is certainly in order.

Some have argued—perhaps out of wishful thinking—that suffering in hell cannot be everlasting. They have advocated what is known as "annihilation." Already at death, some say, the human person goes out of existence completely. This, of course, ignores all that the Bible says about the immortality of the soul created in the image of God.

59. The Bible contrasts everlasting death with everlasting life. Both are eternal—without end. Read again what Jesus says in Matthew 10:28. Read 2 Thessalonians 1:8–10. How is hell described here? What is meant by "destruction"?

60. Read Mark 9:47–48. How is the endless suffering described here?

Because the human soul is immortal, hell begins at death—just as heaven begins at death for believers. Recall Jesus' story about a rich man who had died and found himself in hell. He pleaded to Abraham for his brothers who were still living on earth (Luke 16). Clearly the wicked enter hell right away.

61. Read John 5:28–29. What can you say to those who believe death and the grave are the end, that there is no resurrection?

As with heaven, the exact location of hell is difficult to define. It is not beneath the ground as some ancient pagan religions described it. Spiritual things are beyond our comprehension. The Bible does hint at general directions: Heaven is up, hell is down. But these may simply be examples of God working with people's existing ideas about the universe, not road maps to heaven and hell. The Apostles' Creed states that Jesus "descended into hell" and "ascended into heaven." We do well to leave it at that.

Degrees of Punishment

There is some indication—though no details—that in hell some will receive greater punishment than others.

62. Read Matthew 11:23–24. Which unbelievers can expect the greater punishment (whatever that may be)?

Why Hell?

Unpleasant as the subject is, hell is real. To deny this is to question the truthfulness of Jesus Himself.

63. Why do you think God has revealed this so emphatically? Read 2 Corinthians 6:2.

Hell is little understood. Many have serious doubts about its existence; others blatantly deny that there is a hell. Don't be swayed by this so-called "wisdom" of the unbelieving world. Understand the biblical teaching that the "wages of sin is death" (Romans 6:23). This is much more than physical death. Death, we have seen, is eternal separation from God's love and care in a place called hell.

God, in His love for us sinners, has provided an escape from the tortures of hell: "The free gift of God is eternal life in Christ Jesus our Lord" (Romans 6:23). Thank Him daily for that gift. Remember, too, that God is "not wishing that any should perish, but that all should reach repentance" (2 Peter 3:9). The horrors of hell should cause you to increase your prayers for the lost and your zeal to reach them with the saving Gospel of Christ.

Words to Remember

Whoever believes in the Son has eternal life; whoever does not obey the Son shall not see life, but the wrath of God remains on him. John 3:36

C H A P T E R   F I V E

Living for Heaven

When Tony went to work in a rough-and-tumble lumber mill in the Northwest, he knew it would be a largely unfriendly environment for a Christian. When he returned home after several months, his pastor expressed his concern for Tony, "How did you fare? They probably made it hard for you as a Christian."

Tony seemed rather unconcerned, "It wasn't bad. They haven't found out yet that I am a Christian."

Tony, like many believers, needed to be reminded that heaven-bound people cannot blend in comfortably with the unbelieving world. Our earthly life must reflect that we are citizens of heaven. God in His wisdom foresaw this need and provided for it in the Scriptures. The life in heaven is a continuation and perfection of our spiritual life on earth. In view of the glories of heaven, we need not make the mistake Tony made. God provides the resources needed to help us bear witness to our heavenly Savior.

64. Read 1 Peter 2:11–12. Baptized into Christ, you are on the road to heaven. But how should you see your life now?

With a view toward heaven, we can pinpoint six areas in which a Christian's attitudes and actions reflect a heaven-centered life.

"Let us worship and bow down" (Psalm 95:6)

Heaven is pictured as a worshiping community. Saints, angels, and elders voice their praises to God. It is the dominant activity in heaven.

65. Read Revelation 7:9–12. What is the dominant theme of all worship, whether on earth or in heaven?

Worship is the first and natural response of all who receive the love of God that comes through Jesus Christ. What are we to think of those who have no desire or very little desire to worship God seriously?

66. What kind of worship does Jesus expect of heaven-bound people? Read John 4:24. What do you understand by "in spirit and truth"?

“Born again to a living hope” (1 Peter 1:3)

We may wonder why God has told us so much about the glories of our future life in heaven. He wants us to be hope-filled people on earth. Hope points to your future but gives joy for the present. Christian hope is not mere wishing: “I hope it doesn’t rain tomorrow.” Christian hope is a sure thing.

67. Read 1 Peter 1:3–5. On what fact is your hope based?

The sure hope we have of heaven is a motivating and sustaining force as we live in an imperfect world.

68. Read 1 Peter 1:6–9. In what situations is your hope most helpful?

69. In 1 Peter 3:8–17, the apostle writes about suffering. According to 3:15, how do patient endurance and suffering present opportunities for you?

The road to glory is not always a glorious road, but it does lead to glory. In this hope, God’s people can live and rejoice!

"Set your minds on things that are above" (Colossians 3:2)

If the view of heaven provides a living hope, it must also affect the way you live before you get there. Your mind-set should be one that gives priority to things that are spiritual and eternal. Jesus' miracles show that He is concerned about our temporal needs of food, clothing, shelter, and health, but He often warned against giving priority to them.

70. Read Matthew 6:19–21. In what terms did Jesus present this matter?

We necessarily experience some tensions here: How much time and money to invest in temporal things? How much to "lay away" for a rainy day? We have to begin with the basic principle that "if we have food and clothing, with these we will be content" (1 Timothy 6:8). But beyond that? How are we to distinguish between needs and wants? We know, too, that what we invest in evangelism and world missions bears fruit for eternity, while material things are short-lived. Handling this tension of the earthly vs. the heavenly requires the wisdom of a Solomon!

71. As a group, discuss this tension. Share insights about focusing on earthly and heavenly concerns.

72. What basic insight of Jesus must you always keep before you? Read and discuss Matthew 6:33.

"Love one another" (1 John 4:7)

Another mark of God's heaven-bound people is genuine Christian love that will be perfected in heaven. 1 Corinthians 13 reminds us that love will continue there even after faith and hope are fulfilled. That loving community must have its beginning among Christians on earth.

73. Read Acts 4:32–37. Did the first Christians live up to this expectation? What evidence is there that the early Christians understood and practiced Christian love?

Jesus emphasized that His followers are to be a loving community in the eyes of the world around us.

74. Read John 13:14–15. What does genuine love show to all the world? Do you think the world sees the church in this way today?

We realize, of course, that we are not heaven-bound because of our deeds of love, but we do deeds of love because we are heaven-bound.

75. What has to be your true motivation to show love on earth? Read and discuss 1 John 4:19.

Advent People

"Waiting and watching" is the posture of God's heaven-bound people. They are Advent people waiting for the second coming of the Lord and His ushering in of the final phase of His kingdom. The time may come sooner than we think!

76. Read Revelation 22:20. Can you honestly pray this prayer? Why or why not?

77. The time of Jesus' second coming cannot be known. Read Matthew 24:36 and Acts 1:6–8. Why don't we know the time of Christ's return? What does God want us to know and do?

The signs of the end are all around us: Wars, earthquakes, increasing immorality, teachers of false religions, and so forth. The end of time will come soon, but *soon* is a relative term and simply emphasizes that God's heaven-bound people must be living every day as Advent people expecting Him to appear at any time.

Expect Surprises

Our God is full of surprises and we can be sure that He has kept the greatest surprise of all for the end. The glimpses we have of heaven, wonderful as they are, are necessarily given in terms of our earthly experiences and understanding. Therefore, they are incomplete revelations.

78. Read 1 Corinthians 2:9. What does this tell you about heaven?

God already surprised us with the likes of Christmas, the transfiguration, and Easter. The greatest surprise of all is the Gospel itself—that He would sacrifice His own Son to redeem sinners like us. Expect more surprises when you get to heaven!

As you travel the road that leads to the glories of heaven, welcome God's reminders that the earth is not your permanent home. Recognize your weaknesses and failures as you strive to keep the focus on heavenly things. Confess your faults to God daily. Take advantage of the forgiveness and strength God offers in His Word and Sacraments.

Jesus' death and resurrection gained heaven for you. Through the Gospel, God's Spirit increases your desire and ability to lead the heavenly life now. Though perfection is not possible in your earthly life, growth in faith and Christian life is possible and is expected by your loving God. Pray for His strength to grow more and more like the heaven-bound person He calls you by faith to be. Your worship, love, joy, hope, and Advent attitude will surprise even you!

Words to Remember

Set your minds on things that are above, not on things that are on earth. Colossians 3:2

C H A P T E R   S I X

Curiosity Questions about Heaven

Joey sat with his father. He watched his older brother play Little League baseball. During a lull in the action, he startled his father with a question, "Will I be able to play baseball when I get to heaven? Mommy said that when we get to heaven everything will be perfect."

Joey had been crippled from birth. Joey's father tried to answer tactfully, "I hope so, but God hasn't told us for sure that there will be any baseball in heaven. I'm sure you'll have lots of fun things to do. We'll just have to wait and see."

We are such curious creatures. Such questions about heaven abound, not only from children but also from adults. We need not ignore such questions. Neither should we become overly involved with them. The best approach is to deal with them cautiously, using insights from Scripture.

Activities in Heaven

What can we possibly do for all eternity in heaven? We are activity-oriented beings. Adam and Eve were active in the Garden of Eden before their fall into sin. Fishermen may dream of lakes and rivers, golfers may picture lush golf courses, scholars may think of books and libraries, and so on. But what should we realistically expect?

Earlier we read that worship will be an important activity. This worship may well include portions of the Sunday liturgical services to which we are accustomed. It is certain to be joyful.

What about other possible activities? Since food is so central to our earthly life, we are naturally curious about eating and drinking. The Bible does not discourage us on this matter.

79. Read Matthew 26:29. What does Jesus imply here?

We remember that when we are in heaven we will have a "spiritual body." Will we eat and drink like Jesus did after His resurrection? Obviously there are mysteries to be resolved. Whether in eating and drinking, or any other activity, one thing is certain: there will be no boredom in heaven!

80. Read Revelation 2:26–27 and 3:21. What other activity will the saints participate in?

Relationships

Since relationships are so vital to our earthly life, it is only natural that we are curious about relationships in heaven. Human beings are created to be in happy relationships. Sinful selfishness reeks havoc with our relationships now, but we can be sure that they will be perfectly restored in the glories of heaven. The Scriptures don't give us many details about relationships there.

81. Read Matthew 22:24–30. Does this surprising revelation come as a disappointment or as a relief to married people?

We could probably think of heaven in terms of "one big happy family."

82. Read Acts 2:42–47 where heavenly relationships are best foreshadowed. Which features of this community do you expect to see in heaven?

Recognizing and Knowing Each Other

At Christian funerals we hear of a grand and glorious reunion. Will we recognize each other in heaven? The Scriptures provide only clues and hints, but they are all positive.

83. Read 1 Corinthians 13:12. What does Paul mean by the full knowledge promised here?

At Jesus' transfiguration, Moses and Elijah appeared and were easily recognized by the three disciples. This at least implies that in heaven we too will be able to recognize the believers from biblical times and others who have gone before us into glory. Mysteries remain, but we should not doubt that our knowing as God knows us includes recognizing and enjoying our loved ones.

Pets

Will there be pets in heaven? Will that precious dog, cat, or bird be there for us to enjoy as we did on earth? This is another question to which the Bible gives no direct answer.

84. Several animals or animal-like creatures are pictured as being in heaven or coming from heaven. Read Revelation 4:7; 5:6; and 19:11. What animals are listed? What purpose do they serve in these passages?

Contrary to what evolutionists try to tell us, there is a huge gap between humans, who are created in God's image, and animals created for man's use. We do know that "the resurrection of the body" speaks only of humans. The sentiment that there may be a special "pet heaven" is not taught in the Bible.

Can God possibly recreate a special pet or even create new pets for our enjoyment? We know that with God, all things are possible. Adam and Eve enjoyed animals in the first Paradise before they fell into sin. We do well to leave the whole matter of heavenly pets in God's hands. If they do not appear in glory, it will in no way detract from the glory.

Degrees of Glory

Will the residents of heaven enjoy varying degrees of glory? On this subject again God's Word provides very little information, but does indicate that God may have planned some "rewards of grace."

85. Do you know of any sects or cults which strongly encourage members to work for a higher status in heaven? Share information.

The Bible does not encourage us to think of different levels of heaven. St. Paul does once refer to his having been "caught up to the third heaven" (2 Corinthians 12:2) but he does not encourage us to base a doctrine on that unusual experience. Paul's experience seems to have taken him beyond the visible firmament, and even outer space, into the very presence of God. His experience was so profound and so personal that he was prohibited from revealing all the details.

God made Adam and Eve different. He does dispense special gifts to believers on earth (1 Corinthians 12:11). So God has no problem creating us different from one another. Angels have "ranks" in heaven (e.g., Michael and Gabriel are called "archangels"). We should not imagine that everyone in heaven will appear the same or melt into some amorphous celestial unity.

86. Read Matthew 19:28–29 and Matthew 20:23. What does Jesus imply? What is the difference?

Jesus did not appear to be anxious to elaborate on "degrees of glory." We have also learned that, in heaven, all believers will reign with Jesus as kings. Jesus used earthly terms such as "thrones" and "kingdoms" to describe spiritual realities that are still beyond our comprehension. We do well to wait and see how these special honors are experienced. Above all, there can be no spirit of competition for higher glory among heaven-bound people. Jesus made this plain (Mark 10:42–45).

87. What must be your basic attitude as you look forward to the glories of heaven? Read and discuss 1 Peter 5:6.

Curiosity about heaven will always be with us. This is not bad. God does not fault you for being curious about the unknown things of heaven, but He does ask you to let it be controlled and limited and to keep your focus on the sure things He has revealed in His Word.

The important questions about heaven are answered. The way to heaven—most important of all—is clear and certain. The kingdom of heaven is open to all believers in Jesus. He atoned for their sins by His sacrificial death on the cross and His victorious resurrection. The Bible's pictures of heaven, many of them in symbolic language, portray a future life of joy and honor that has no end. This is the heaven God wants you to enjoy. Already you have a taste of that joy as you live your new life in Christ by the power of the Holy Spirit. Your worship and love foreshadow what will be perfected in heaven. As a stranger and pilgrim on earth, you enjoy your earthly blessings, but always live in joyful anticipation of that glorious future God has planned for you as His gift through Jesus Christ.

Words to Remember

I press on toward the goal for the prize of the upward call of God in Christ Jesus. Philippians 3:14

Leader Notes

This guide is provided as a "safety net," a place to turn for help in answering questions and enriching discussion. It will not answer every question raised in your class. Please read it, along with the questions, before class. Consult it in class only after exploring the Bible references and discussing what they teach. Please note the different abilities of your class members. Some will easily find the Bible passages listed in this study; others will struggle. To make participation easier, team up members of the class. For example, if a question asks you to look up several passages, assign one passage to one group, the second to another, and so on. Divide the work! Let participants present the answers they discover.

Each topic is divided into four sections:

Focus introduces the topic for discussion.

Science critique summarizes what modern science has discovered about the topic.

Law critique considers the topic in view of God's commands.

Gospel affirmation helps students understand how God addresses the issues raised by the topic through His Son, Jesus Christ.

C H A P T E R   O N E

There Is a Heaven—Really!

Objectives: By the power of the Holy Spirit working through God's Word, participants will be reconvinced that heaven is real and awaits all who believe in Jesus, and they will look forward to our future lessons on heaven.

1. Let participants share their thoughts briefly. Take note of people's ideas about heaven and where their ideas come from. Some ideas will correctly reflect what the Bible teaches, but others may not. Don't take time to address all the issues yet. Summarize this activity by emphasizing that this study will help people discover what God says about heaven.

2. The promise of heaven offers comfort in time of bereavement and a challenge to live a godly life on earth.

3. The writers of Scripture did not attempt to answer every question about life or the afterlife. The main purpose of Scripture is to help us know Jesus for eternal life. For other matters, we can trust that God has revealed all we need to know now in His Word.

Exploring Life after Death

4. Death is not the end and cannot separate us from a glorious life in heaven. God's love for us in Christ Jesus transcends every natural and supernatural experience.

5. Such experiences may be genuine. Scientists have difficulty confirming or denying them. The fact that so many people have such experiences could indicate that there is life beyond the physical things we experience.

6. Answers will vary. Participants familiar with the media should

be able to give examples of secular ridicule of the Christian belief in heaven, as well as gross distortions and misconceptions of that belief.

7. Life in heaven should be our ultimate goal. Its promise affects how we live upon the earth. The surety of Christ's resurrection gives us hope and courage even in this life. Because of Him, we look forward to our own resurrection.

8. Answers may vary. In most situations even those who look forward to heaven are not anxious to leave behind their life on earth. Life on earth seems too precious. Relationships here are treasured. For most, heaven seems nebulous and far away. (Exceptions may be those who are terminally ill.)

9. Participants should express honest feelings. Wanting to go to heaven or stay on earth can be rooted in selfishness. Discuss how, like Paul, we may continue to serve others through a longer life. We always serve our brothers and sisters at our Lord's pleasure.

10. Atheists, agnostics, and those believing in reincarnation reject the clear, authoritative teachings of the Bible that humans are created in God's image, that we are fallen by nature, and that Jesus came to rescue us from eternal death and give to us eternal life.

11. Revealed to His servant John, the promises in Revelation are God's truth. As surely as God lives and speaks, there is a life in heaven for all who believe in His Son, Jesus. This truth is a tremendous source of comfort and joy.

12. We should and can be convinced of heaven and freed of doubts by continuing in God's Word and Sacraments. Read John 8:31–32. Through the Word, written and proclaimed, and the promises of Baptism and Absolution, the Lord uplifts and encourages us. In the Lord's Supper, we literally taste the very joys and comforts of heaven itself, given to us in Christ's true body and true blood.

CHAPTER TWO

Popular Misconceptions

Objectives: By the power of the Holy Spirit working through God's Word, participants will recognize popular but misleading conceptions of heaven and focus on what the Bible actually reveals about our future life in heaven.

13. Answers will vary. Don't squelch input by trying to correct misunderstandings here or by harshly criticizing them. Move participants into the questions and Scripture passages. The Word changes hearts and minds.

Heaven Is for Everybody

14. God is love, but He is also holy and just. His plan is that only those who receive His love in Christ will be saved. Unfortunately, even some Christians are swayed by the opinion that a loving God will not send sinners to a fiery hell. This view of Scripture and of Christ is inherently one-sided and inconsistent with all of the teachings of the Bible and of Christ Himself.

15. Ultimately we will be able to distinguish believers from unbelievers only when Christ returns on the Judgment Day.

16. He will clearly divide the righteous and the wicked from one another. He will base His judgment on each person's faith, which produces the righteous or unrighteous works described here. Note the description of the righteous: they are blessed by the Father with genuine faith (Matthew 16:16–17). In view of faith, they produced genuine good works. Without faith, unbelievers, then, produced no good works at all.

Heaven Is for Good People

17. No one is good enough to earn heaven. Everyone breaks God's Law. Paul explains that our righteousness, our right relationship with God, comes only through faith in His Son, Jesus Christ. James explains that breaking one commandment shatters the entire Law. This is similar to throwing a rock against one part of a window, but shattering the entire thing. Paul and James both teach that we are saved by grace through faith, which results in good works (see Ephesians 2:8–10).

18. We are good enough for heaven only by God's mercy. God declares us righteous through faith in Jesus Christ, who paid the price for our sins, freeing us from the curse of condemnation and doubt.

19. If we reject God's Gospel of salvation in Jesus Christ alone, we have no Gospel at all and remain under the curse of the Law.

Heaven Is on Earth

20. Such a belief denies that man, unlike animals, is created in God's image with an immortal soul that cannot die. It also denies the necessity of a final judgment on good and evil (Revelation 20:11–15), which the Scriptures, and to an extent even human experience, prove cannot be obtained "on earth."

Heaven Is Merely a Condition

21. Jesus emphasized that heaven is a real place by comparing it to a house with many rooms. God did not create us as mental or physical beings only. He created us body and soul. Therefore, He will save us body and soul. See 2 Corinthians 5:1–10, where Paul compares the body to a tent or dwelling for the soul.

From Heaven They Smile Down on Us

22. The Bible says little about what people in heaven may know about intimate, earthly affairs. Ecclesiastes 9:5 and Isaiah 63:16 seem to indicate that the souls of dead believers do not possess omniscience—knowledge of all things—which is a divine attribute. On the other hand, Revelation 6:9–10 and Luke 16:27 suggest that they may have some knowledge as to earthly transactions.

23. God communicates to us through His revealed Word, which contains all we need to know now. Any claims that God communicates with individuals in other ways must be judged on the basis of what the written Word tells us.

In Heaven We Become Angels

24. For a human being, becoming an angel would be a demotion. Angels are only messengers, while believers are sons and daughters of God. In fact, the angels long to understand the promise of salvation for us in Christ (1 Peter 1:12). The divine Son of God assumed not angelic nature, but human nature—a real human body and a rational human soul.

25. Believers are "fellow heirs with Christ" (Romans 8:17) inheriting with Him everything that belongs to God.

26. Although we will never be angels, we will be close to God with everlasting innocence, righteousness, and blessedness, and we will continually praise and worship Him in heaven.

St. Peter Guards the Pearly Gates

27. Peter, as spokesman for all the disciples, is given the "keys of the kingdom" (Matthew 16:19). Some have concluded from this that Peter would control the "pearly gates." The Bible explains else-

where that the power to "open" heaven for others—the forgiveness of sins through the Gospel—is given to the whole church and exercised through the pastoral office (see Matthew 18:18; John 20:21–23).

28. Jesus Himself.

29. The "gatekeeper" is the door Himself, Jesus Christ. He is the only way to the Father (John 14:6).

C H A P T E R T H R E E

Pictures of Heaven

Objectives: By the power of the Holy Spirit, through God's Word, participants will experience the joys of anticipating the glories of heaven and be motivated to increase their thanksgiving and service to God in response to this glorious promise.

30. The attempts by artists or filmmakers to picture heaven should assure us that heaven is a glorious place in God's presence. However, any attempt to illustrate heaven surely fails in comparison to the glory we will experience in heaven as we enjoy the immediate presence of God and Christ.

Paradise

31. Participants should notice that paradise is not described except for the fact that the thief and Jesus will be there together. Perhaps Jesus was drawing on common Jewish understandings from Scripture (see Genesis 2:8–10) that the final paradise will be like a garden.

32. Paul himself does not seem to fully understand his experience. The purpose of it was not to show him everything that goes on in heaven. It is quite possible that human language simply cannot express Paul's experience.

The Father's House

33. Participants should be encouraged to discuss Jesus' image of a house with many rooms and then be directed to the explanations given in the lesson.

34. The house of David included the entire tribe or kingdom of Judah. The house of Saul included the entire tribe of Benjamin. Thus, a house implies completeness or fullness.

The Holy City

35. Answers will vary. Most participants will realize that Revelation is largely symbolic (e.g., certainly Jesus is not an actual lamb with seven horns and seven eyes as described in Revelation 5:6). The explanations that follow should be helpful.

Rest

36. True rest is being with Jesus and free of all earthly troubles.

37. This promise mentions only that in heaven we are at rest from our earthly sufferings. The blessing includes much more: being in heaven with God.

38. The rest given to believers at death is being in God's presence, where there is perfect relaxation and peace.

39. In heaven we will be at rest, but we won't be couch potatoes. There, we will continually celebrate God's grace in Christ in song and worship.

Forever with the Lord

40. When Christ returns for the final time on the Last Day, believers, both the living and the dead, will be "caught up" to join Him. Our life with Christ in perfect, resurrected bodies will be eternal, which is the point Paul is making to comfort the Thessalonians and us.

41. Paul contrasts his service on earth with his rest in heaven. He also wrestles over which he prefers. In the end, he trusts that God will decide the time for his departure.

42. Paul concludes that whether in heaven or on earth, his life is one of service to his neighbor.

The Crown of Life

43. Hear opinions. Wearing the crown means in some way ruling with Christ.

44. In the Olympic games and in athletic events during biblical times, winners were often rewarded with crowns of laurel. In a few short weeks, these would dry out and eventually have to be discarded. In contrast, our crowns are eternal.

I Shall Know Fully

45. Hear opinions. Mysteries may be the Holy Trinity and all of those "why" questions that come up in our life on earth.

46. God will share His knowledge with us and we'll see Him as He is.

A Spiritual Body

47. Hear opinions. Although the words seem contradictory, Paul is expressing a deep, spiritual truth. Our real bodies will be resurrected like Christ's body. How this will happen, we do not know. What we do know is this: what is resurrected will not be just "spirit," but our glorified, earthly frame.

48. Note the struggle to describe "spiritual body." Paul uses the language of planting and harvesting, as though describing a crop that will never rot or lose its usefulness.

49. Participants will recognize that our bodies will be like the glorified body of Jesus after His resurrection. To be glorified like Jesus—that will be heaven!

CHAPTER FOUR

That Other Place

Objectives: By the power of the Holy Spirit through the Word of God, participants will understand the reality and horror of hell and be motivated to better appreciate God's gift of heaven through Christ.

50. Answers may vary. Perhaps some people have no understanding of the horror of hell. Perhaps others do not believe that it exists.

51. Even believers may not take the reality of hell seriously. Also, hell is difficult to talk about if you believe that someone you know might go there. Fear of ridicule for believing in such "old-fashioned ideas" may keep us from speaking (or preaching) about hell.

The Reality of Hell

52. The God of great love is also righteous and just and cannot close His eyes to sin and unbelief. Christianity that has been influenced by the New Age movement (itself influenced by Hinduism) often minimizes or rejects the concepts of God's righteousness and justice.

53. God does not force people to go to hell, but does *let* them go there if they reject His love and forgiveness in Christ.

54. Those who go to hell are cursed. Hell was originally prepared as a prison for the devil and his angels. It is eternal and fiery. Jesus knows the reality and horror of hell. In His love and concern for people, He warns against unbelief and its consequences. We, too, should warn others of hell.

55. The teaching about hell should strike fear in their hearts and make them ready for the Gospel.

56. As believers, we should realize that we were headed for hell because of our sins, and we are rescued from hell through hearing and believing the Gospel of Christ.

What, Where, and When

57. Speaking through Peter, God calls unbelievers to repent of their sins, and be baptized into Christ for the forgiveness of their sins. This promise of forgiveness through Baptism, incorporation into Christ, and the gift of the Holy Spirit, is for all people, including infants and children.

58. The Scriptures depict hell as separation from God's gracious presence, in eternal fire, utter darkness, and intense physical and spiritual agony (weeping and gnashing teeth).

59. Destruction is not easily defined. Words like *incapacitated* or *ruined* come to mind. It is not annihilation. Hell is destruction that lasts forever, as well as total separation from God's love and care.

60. Endless suffering is like a wiggling worm that suffers in the flames but never dies.

61. After death, the scoffers will have no choice but to accept biblical reality. Everyone will rise for the judgment.

Degrees of Punishment

62. Those who have had the greatest opportunities to know Jesus and rejected Him—like those in Capernaum where Jesus lived—can expect the greatest severity of hell.

Why Hell?

63. The doctrine of hell is explicit and uncompromising so that unbelievers will repent and believe, and so that we Christians proclaim the Gospel of salvation to rescue them from hell.

CHAPTER FIVE

Living for Heaven

Objectives: By the power of the Holy Spirit through the Word of God, participants will realize that they are already citizens of heaven, and that their lives on earth must reflect that in their attitudes and actions.

64. As God's holy people and royal priests (see 1 Peter 2:9–10), we are temporary residents on earth, passing through on our way to heaven.

"Let us worship and bow down" (Psalm 95:6)

65. The dominant theme for worship is thanking and praising God our Father for salvation through Jesus Christ, given to us by the Holy Spirit.

66. Hear opinions. Worship must be directed to the only true God—Father, Son, and Holy Spirit—and must come from the heart. In John's Gospel the truth is always associated with the person and teachings of Jesus.

"Born again to a living hope" (1 Peter 1:3)

67. Our hope is based on the reality of Christ's resurrection from the dead. According to Peter, our new birth (1:3) through the Word (1:23) occurred at our Baptism into Christ's resurrection (3:21).

68. The hope that is ours through our Baptism into Christ helps us in times of suffering and disappointment. With Christ and in Christ there is hope for the future.

69. Peter says that in endurance and suffering the door is open to speak of our faith in Christ and pray that others will come to faith (evangelism).

"Set your minds on things that are above" (Colossians 3:2)

70. Jesus teaches that heaven is a treasure much more valuable than any earthly treasure.

71. Encourage individuals to share what works for them (or does not work) in stewardship matters. Assure them that this struggle requires much prayer and reflection on God's Word. Through His grace, God strengthens us in our vocations as we choose, plan, and decide.

72. We may resolve that spiritual things have top priority in our lives and to trust God to provide the material things we need.

"Love one another" (1 John 4:7)

73. Sharing material blessings seemed to come naturally for the first Christians as they appreciated God's love for them. Examples could be drawn from modern life as well.

It should also be noted that the saints in Jerusalem later fell on hard times, and offerings had to be gathered to support them (2 Corinthians 9). God grants us generous hearts and thoughtful minds like the Christians in ancient Jerusalem and Corinth as we work together toward the goals of His kingdom!

74. Genuine love shows that we belong to Jesus and want to love as He loved. (The world sees some of this but probably not enough.)

75. God's love to us in sending His Son to be our Savior is the true source of our motivation. His love for us in Christ overflows in our love for our neighbor.

Advent People

76. Ask for opinions. Most will probably agree that not many people are praying for Judgment Day to come tomorrow.

77. God knows the time but says it's not for us to know. He wants us to live as Advent people, alert and watching every day. He calls us to proclaim the Gospel throughout the world while we wait, watch, and pray.

Expect Surprises

78. In this verse, Paul tells us that the glories of heaven are beyond our present understanding.

C H A P T E R   S I X

Curiosity Questions about Heaven

Objectives: By the power of the Holy Spirit working through God's Word, participants will understand that God has revealed all we need to know about heaven at this time, and that He cultivates in us a "wait and see" attitude.

Activities in Heaven

79. Jesus implies that there will be some kind of eating and drinking. The numerous parables and references to banquets in the heavenly kingdom suggest joyful feasting and drinking.

80. In both passages, Jesus states that we will rule with Him in heaven.

Relationships

81. A few humorous comments may be expected here. Marriage, of course, is a blessing for earthly life and a necessity for the bearing and raising of children. This will no longer be necessary in heaven.

Jesus' statement about marriage does answer a question twice-married people may have, "Which one will it be in heaven?" Apparently, sexual attraction or gender differences will not be a factor.

82. No one will be poor, needy, hungry, or sick. The Word and Sacrament, so essential here on earth, will no longer be necessary—we will be in the immediate presence of God and the Lamb. Unity and love will continue to be expressed.

Recognizing and Knowing Each Other

83. Full knowledge means to know and understand as God now does and we do not. We can expect mysteries to be solved and our many "Why?" questions to be answered.

Pets

84. Lion, ox, eagle, lamb, and horse. The animals or animal features serve as symbols of heavenly characteristics. For example, the lamb stands for Christ, who offered Himself for our sins. These passages neither prove nor disprove the place of animals in heaven.

Degrees of Glory

85. Some may know that the Mormons and Jehovah's Witnesses are two groups that emphasize this (see *Comparative Views on Life After Death*).

86. Jesus emphasized that we should never think in terms of power over others. Special positions in heaven would have to be positions of grace.

87. We are not to seek honor, but trust that God will bestow honors in His way and His time.

Biblical Terms for Heaven and Hell

(adapted from *Christian Cyclopedia*, Concordia Publishing House, © 1984)

Abyssos, Abyss. *Abyssos* is a Greek word meaning "bottomless, unbounded." It means (1) the "deep," or primeval waters (Genesis 1:2); (2) the depths of the earth as a symbol of great distress and anguish of soul (Psalm 71:20); (3) the abode of the dead (Romans 10:7); and (4) hell, as Apollyon's abode over evil spirits (Revelation 9:1–2, 11; 11:7; 17:8; 20:1, 3).

Gehenna. Gehenna is the Greek name of a deep, narrow valley, which runs southwest alongside Jerusalem and wraps around its south end. In this valley, wicked Israelites sacrificed children to the Canaanite idol Molech ("Valley of...Hinnom" in 2 Kings 23:10). Later, the valley was used for burning refuse. Because of its sordid past, Gehenna came to refer to the abode of the wicked after death (Matthew 5:22, 29; 10:28; Mark 9:43, 45; Luke 12:5; James 3:6).

Hades. *Hades* may come from the Greek word for "unseen." In non-biblical Greek literature, it means the realm of the dead. In the Greek translation of the Old Testament (Septuagint), *Hades* is used almost exclusively for ***Sheol.*** In the New Testament, it means "realm of the dead" (Acts 2:27, 31; Revelation 20:13–14) or a place where unbelievers, like the rich man, suffer (Luke 16:23).

Heaven. Heaven is (1) the sky with everything in it (Hebrews 1:10; Matthew 16:2); (2) outer space (Hebrews 11:12); (3) the dwelling place of God, Christ, and the angels, and our heavenly home (Matthew 5:12; 5:34; 18:10; 23:22; 24:26; Acts 1:9–11; 7:49; 1 Peter 1:4).

Paradise. *Paradise*, perhaps a Persian word, can mean (1) a garden or park, for example, the Garden of Eden (Genesis 2:8–17); (2) the heavenly paradise, home of God's saints (Luke 23:43; 2 Corinthians 12:3; Revelation 2:7).

Sheol. *Sheol* occurs sixty-five times in the Hebrew Old Testament. Scholars still struggle to understand it. Martin Luther translated it as "hell" in all places except Genesis 37:35; 42:38; 44:29, 31. In these passages he translated it as "grave." The King James translators used "grave," "hell," and "pit." Since the origin of the word is uncertain, the context must determine the meaning in each case.

Sheol may mean the resting place of man's mortal remains (Job 17:16; Isaiah 38:10), or the "realm of the dead" (e.g., Genesis 37:35; Job 7:9; Psalm 16:10; 31:17; 89:48). In this sense *sheol* is very much like the English expressions "the hereafter" or "the beyond." Going "down to Sheol" means "to die, to depart from the land of the living." But it should be noted that when the righteous are said to descend into Sheol, their fate beyond is never taken into account. The hope of the pious in the Old Testament is expressed differently (e.g., Psalm 73:24).

Sheol may mean the place where evildoers face God's judgment. Sheol receives people taken away in God's anger, such as Korah's rebel band (Numbers 16:30, 33) and harlots (Proverbs 5:5). The Lord's anger burns to the depths of Sheol (Deuteronomy 32:22). According to Psalm 49, all people die physically, righteous as well as ungodly (v. 10). But there is a difference in their existence in the hereafter. The psalmist confidently expresses, "They [i.e. the wicked] are laid in the grave [Sheol], death shall feed on them… but God will redeem my soul from the power of the grave [Sheol], for He shall receive me" (Psalm 49:14–15 KJV). Clearly there is a sharp contrast between the doom of the ungodly and the glorious hope of the believer, who hopes to rest securely in the hands of God. (See also Psalm 73.)

Tartaros. The Greek word *Tartaros* is not in the Bible, but a related verb form occurs in 2 Peter 2:4. In Greek mythology, Tartaros is an underground prison, regarded as the abode of the wicked dead where they suffer punishment for their evil deeds; it corresponds to **Gehenna** as a name for hell.

Comparative Views on Life after Death

Faith Group	Death	Body
Lutheran	Temporal and spiritual death results from the fall. Temporal death separates soul from body.	The body is an important part of God's creation. It is laid to rest until the resurrection on the Last Day.
Conservative Protestant	Temporal and spiritual death results from the fall. Temporal death separates soul from body.	The body is an important part of God's creation. It is laid to rest until the resurrection.
Eastern Orthodox	Temporal death and spiritual impairment results from the fall. Soul and body separate at death.	The body is an important part of God's creation. It is laid to rest until the resurrection on the Last Day.
Roman Catholic	Temporal death and spiritual impairment results from the fall. Soul and body separate at death.	The body is an important part of God's creation. It is laid to rest until the resurrection on the Last Day.
Liberal Protesant	Death occurs naturally as a part of physical existence. An afterlife may or may not exist.	The human body holds value only in so far as it supports painless, productive human existence.
Jewish	Range from end of bodily life and entrance into "the world to come," to an end of all existence.	The body is an important part of God's creation.

Soul	Resurrection	Heaven & Hell
Souls of believers immediately go to heaven. Souls of unbelievers immediately go to hell.	The souls of all the dead will be rejoined with their earthly bodies at the resurrection on the Last Day.	Believers spend eternity in a new heaven and earth. Unbelievers spend eternity in the torments of hell.
Souls of believers immediately go to heaven. Souls of unbelievers immediately go to hell.	The souls of all the dead will be rejoined with their earthly bodies at the resurrection (or resurrections).	Believers spend eternity in a new heaven and earth. Unbelievers spend eternity in the torments of hell.
Souls of believers doing good works go to heaven. Other souls go to hell.	The souls of all the dead will be rejoined with their earthly bodies at the resurrection on the Last Day.	Believers doing good works go to the new heaven. Others, separated from God, go to the new earth.
Perfect souls go to heaven. Imperfect souls spend time in purgatory. Souls in mortal sin go to hell.	The souls of all the dead will be rejoined with their earthly bodies at the resurrection on the Last Day.	Those doing good works spend eternity in a new heaven and earth. Those in mortal sin go to hell.
The "soul" is a person's cognitive and emotive abilities and/or spiritual aspirations.	The "resurrection" is best expressed as improving human life through Jesus' ethical teachings.	All people will be "saved," if only through their memories being preserved by their loved ones.
We are made in God's image with the capacity to choose good or evil.	Wide range of beliefs including bodily resurrection.	Orthodox: reward or punishment in heaven or hell. Liberal: denial of afterlife.

Faith Group	Death	Body
Mormon	The fall opened the way for Gospel and ordinances. Death separates soul from body.	Procreation is encouraged because God's pre-existent spirit children need earthly bodies.
Jehovah's Witness	Cessation of both soul and bodily life.	The body is an important part of God's creation.
Muslim	Death separates soul from body.	The body is an important part of Allah's creation. It is laid to rest until the resurrection.
Hindu	Basic human condition is samsara, the cycle of birth and death.	Physical body has little worth.
Buddhist	Human condition is suffering, caused by the attachment and desire for material things.	Attachment to the physical body is actually a hindrance to achieving nirvana.
Secular Humanist	Man is part of nature. Death is a natural process in which man participates.	Body serves no purpose after death.

Soul	Resurrection	Heaven & Hell
Pre-existent children of God; gods-in-embryo with the potential of achieving godhood.	Teaches a general, bodily resurrection for all the dead.	Only the best Mormons go to the Celestial Kingdom. Only the worst sinners go to the Outer Darkness.
Created in Jehovah's image, although the soul is not immortal.	No literal resurrection, but at the end Jehovah will re-create all but the most wicked.	144,000 "elect" Witnesses go to heaven; others go to paradise. Those rejecting Jehovah face annihilation.
Humans created basically pure, although fallible and in need of Allah's guidance. Soul immortal.	Teaches a general, bodily resurrection for all the dead.	Faithful Muslims go to Paradise. Non-Muslims and those who commit shirk (apostasy) go to a fiery hell.
The soul is immortal, part of Brahman. People unaware that they themselves are "God."	No resurrection. Goal of life is to obtain final release, or moksha, from reincarnation.	Cycles of reincarnation (birth, death) until one is absorbed into Brahman, the Ultimate Reality.
Denies existence of the "self" apart from physical and mental attributes.	No resurrection. Goal of life is nirvana (negation of suffering), achieved only by eliminating desire.	May pass through a series of heavens and hells on the way to achieving nirvana.
The "soul" ceases to exist at bodily death.	No resurrection.	"Heaven" can only mean the improvement of man's condition through science and technology.

Glossary

agnosticism. A philosophical view that any knowledge of the supernatural—God, creation, the afterlife—is incomplete, or has not been reached. Agnosticism does not reject the possibility that Deity may indeed exist.

annihilationism. The belief that God will annihilate—cause to cease to exist—the souls of the unrighteous after death. This unbiblical view is taught by the "Christian" cult, the Jehovah's Witnesses.

atheism. The belief that no supreme being exists outside of the physical universe. Ironically, because atheism is dogmatic (insistent that its beliefs are absolutely true), it may be considered a "religion."

eschatology. Literally, "the study of last things," referring to the end of the world. In theology, eschatology deals with the topics of death, the reappearing of Christ, judgment, and eternal life.

Gnosticism. An early heresy (whose teachings are promoted by some modern "Christian" cults), which disparaged the created material world. Gnosticism denied that Jesus had a physical body. John refers to Gnostic teachers as "antichrists" (1 John 2:18; 4:3).

Gospel. The message of Christ's life, death, and resurrection for the forgiveness of sins. The Holy Spirit works through the Gospel to create faith and convert people.

hyper-spiritualism, hyper-spirituality. In this study, excessive interest in or focus on the spiritual world to the depreciation, if not exclusion, of the material world. Hyper-spirituality may deny the incarnation of the Son of God in human flesh or His bodily resurrection, pit personal religious "revelation" or "experience" against the concrete means of grace (Word and Sacraments), stress God's miracles at the expense of God's regular work in the created order, or de-emphasize (or reject) the bodily resurrection of the dead while promoting post-death "spiritual" existence. See **Gnosticism.**

incarnation. From the Latin "in the flesh." It refers to the conception of Jesus, God the Son, in the womb of the Virgin Mary by the Holy Spirit. Do not confuse incarnation with **reincarnation**, a Hindu doctrine.

intermediate state of souls. The Roman Catholic Church teaches that when people die, their souls may go to places other than heaven or hell. Instead, they may go to limbo (unbaptized infants) or purgatory (those who have not attained perfection in this life). Other denominations have held that the soul of a dead person does not go to heaven, but rests in the ground with the body until the resurrection ("soul sleep").

Law. God's will which shows people how they should live (e.g., the Ten Commandments) and condemns their failure. The preaching of the Law is the cause of contrition (genuine sorrow over sin).

means of grace. The means by which God gives us forgiveness, life, and salvation, won by the life, death, and resurrection of Jesus Christ: the Gospel and the Sacraments.

naturalism. Philosophical worldview maintaining that nothing exists beyond the world of nature and material realities.

New Age. The eclectic blend of religious and cultural beliefs, customs, and attitudes arising in the twentieth century and later, which emphasizes reincarnation, alternative spiritualities, and health.

nihilism. From the Latin, *nihilo* (nothing); a philosophical worldview denying the existence of an afterlife and/or any ultimate accountability such as God.

reincarnation. The Hindu teaching that after death the life force, or soul, of the deceased transmigrates to other bodies, including human, plant, or animal. The cycle of birth, death, and rebirth occurs until the soul merges with Brahman, the Ultimate Reality. Many **New Age** beliefs are based on Hindu teachings.

Sacrament. Literally, something sacred. In the Lutheran church, a Sacrament is a sacred act that (1) was instituted by Christ, (2) has a visible, earthly element, and (3) offers the forgiveness of sins earned by Christ. The Sacraments include Holy Baptism, Holy Communion, and Holy Absolution (if one counts the pastor as the visible element).

spirituality. Personal religious interest or sensitivity; recognizing that more than the material world exists.